How we USE materials

Glass

Holly Wallace

W
FRANKLIN WATTS

First published in 2006 by
Franklin Watts
338 Euston Road
London NW1 3BH

Franklin Watts Australia
Hachette Children's Books
Level 17/207 Kent Street
Sydney NSW 2000

Art director: Jonathan Hair
Series designed and created for Franklin Watts by Painted Fish Ltd.
Designer: Rita Storey
Editor: Fiona Corbridge

Picture credits:
Corbis/James L. Amos p. 27 (bottom); Hilary Green, Dartington Crystal,
Torrington, Devon, England, p. 8, p. 9; istockphoto.com p. 10, p. 12, p. 13, p. 14,
p. 15, p. 16, p. 17 (top), p. 18 (right), p. 19, p. 20, p. 21, p. 22, p. 24 (bottom), p. 25,
p. 26, p. 27 (top); Tudor Photography p. 3, p. 5, p. 6, p. 7, p. 11, p. 17 (bottom),
p. 18 (left), p. 23, p. 24 (top).

Cover images: Tudor Photography, Banbury

ISBN-10: 0 7496 6459 2
ISBN-13: 978 0 7496 6459 6
Dewey classification: 666'.1

A CIP catalogue record for this book is available from the British Library.

Printed in China

Contents

Words in **bold** are in the glossary.

What is glass?

Glass is a **material**. We use it to make all sorts of different things.

Look around you. How many things can you see that are made of glass?

● This window and vase are made of glass. Glass is **transparent**. This means that you can see through it.

Glass feels very smooth, like these marbles.

Glass is **waterproof** and **airtight**, so it is good for making jars to store food.

Light bulbs are made of glass because it lets light shine through it and it does not melt when it gets warm.

Glass keywords
Material
Transparent
Waterproof
Airtight

Where does glass come from?

Glass is not a **natural** material. It is made in factories and then turned into objects.

Glass is mostly made from sand and a rock called **limestone**. The sand and limestone are mixed with **chemicals** and turn into a white powder.

The mixture is heated until it melts. The liquid glass is poured into different **moulds** to make glass objects and shapes.

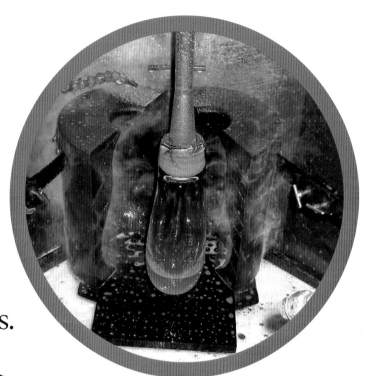

Glass can be shaped in another way. A **glassblower** puts a blob of **molten** glass on the end of a tube. Then he blows down the tube to blow up the glass like a balloon.

Glass keywords
Sand
Limestone
Glassblower
Molten

What is glass like?

When molten glass cools into a shape, it stays in that shape. Glass is a hard material.

Glass can be made into lots of different shapes. We use flat sheets of glass to make windows.

Glass is waterproof, so liquid cannot soak through it. We use glass to make **containers** for liquid, such as this jug and glasses.

Glass is **brittle** and can break if it is dropped. Pieces of broken glass are very sharp.

Glass keywords

Brittle
Sharp

Windows

Glass used in windows and doors is called **glazing**. The glass is fixed into frames made from wood, metal or plastic.

Glass is good for windows because it lets sunlight shine through it but keeps rain and wind out. Glass also keeps warm air in.

● In cold countries, windows often have two sheets of glass with a small gap between them. This is called **double glazing**. It makes buildings warmer.

● The glass in many bathroom windows has a rough surface. It is called **frosted glass**. It is **opaque**, which means it lets light in but people cannot see through it.

Glass keywords

Glazing
Double glazing
Frosted glass

13

Glass in buildings

Glass is a good material for using in buildings because it is strong and lets light in.

Some buildings, such as this skyscraper, are covered in glass. This type of covering is called a curtain wall. This is because the glass hangs outside the building like a large curtain.

Some walls and doors are made of glass, too. They let light through to make a room lighter. This wall is made from glass bricks.

Glass **greenhouses** are used for growing plants in. The glass traps the Sun's heat. The heat and light help the plants to grow.

Glass keywords
Light
Greenhouse

Mirrors and lights

We use glass to make beautiful mirrors and lights for our homes. These are useful and nice to look at.

A mirror is made from a sheet of glass. The back of the glass is covered in silver paint. Light goes into the mirror and bounces off the paint and out again. That is how you can see yourself.

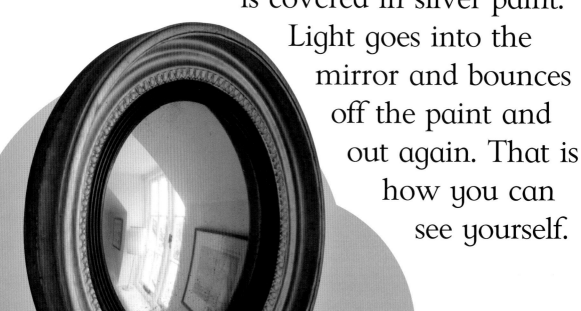

A chandelier is a light that has many tiny pieces of glass. The glass sparkles when the light is turned on.

This lamp is made of special glass fibres called **optical fibres**. Light from a light bulb at one end travels along the fibres and comes out at the other end.

Glass keywords

Mirror
Optical fibres
Light bulb

Containers

Glass containers are made in moulds. They can be many different shapes.

- Glass is waterproof, so it is good for making bottles, jars and drinking glasses. It is also **long-lasting**. Glass containers can be washed and used again.

We can store food in glass jars because glass is airtight. This means air cannot make the food go **mouldy**.

Bowls and dishes used for cooking are made from special glass. This type of glass does not crack if it is heated up, so it can be used to cook food in a hot oven.

Glass keywords

Container

Long-lasting

Glass for seeing

Did you know that pieces of curved glass can help you to see things better?

The pieces of glass in spectacles are called **lenses**. The lenses are curved, so they bend light. This helps people with poor eyesight to see better.

A **magnifying glass** has a lens which is thicker in the middle than at the edges. It bends light to make things look bigger than they actually are.

The lenses in a **microscope** work in the same way. They are so powerful that you can see tiny objects which are otherwise too small to see.

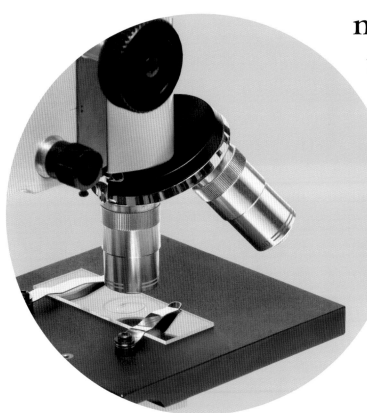

Glass keywords

Lenses
Magnifying
Curved

Glass for decoration

Many beautiful objects are made from coloured or **decorated** glass.

To make glass in different colours, special chemicals are added. The coloured glass is called **stained glass**. This stained-glass window is made from many pieces of coloured glass.

Because glass can be made in different shapes and colours, it is good for making **ornaments**, like these paperweights.

Glass sparkles and looks pretty when light shines through it. Glass can be made into beads, like those on this bracelet.

Glass keywords

Sparkles

Stained glass

Glass in transport

The windows of planes, cars, and buses are made of special **safety glass**.

- Safety glass is very tough and does not break as easily as ordinary glass. If it does get broken in an accident, it shatters into lots of tiny pieces. These pieces are not as dangerous as bigger pieces of **jagged** glass.

The mirrors on this motorbike are made from mirror glass. They allow the rider to see traffic behind the motorbike.

This kayak is made from **fibreglass**. Fibreglass is a very strong and hard-wearing material.

Glass keywords
Safety glass
Hard-wearing
Fibreglass

Recycling glass

We throw away millions of glass bottles and jars every day. But the glass in rubbish dumps does not **rot**.

Instead of throwing away used glass bottles and jars, we can collect them and put them in special **recycling** bins. The glass can be made into new glass objects.

Objects that can be recycled have this **logo** on them.

The glass is taken to a recycling factory. It is crushed and melted to make new glass. Here you can see the crushed glass ready for recycling.

Nearly all glass objects we use today contain some recycled glass.

Glass keywords
Recycling
Crushed
Melted

Glossary

Airtight Does not let air pass through it.

Brittle A material that is hard but breaks easily when it is dropped.

Chemicals Special substances used to do many jobs, including making glass.

Containers Objects such as jars or bottles, used for holding or carrying things.

Decorated Something that has had a pattern or picture added to make it look more attractive.

Double glazing Windows made from two layers of glass. They help to keep buildings warm.

Fibreglass A material made from very thin threads of glass mixed with plastic.

Frosted glass Glass with a rough surface.

Glassblower Someone who makes glass objects by blowing through a tube into molten glass.

Glazing Sheets of glass in windows and doors.

Greenhouses Sheds with glass roofs and walls, for growing plants in.

Jagged Having sharp, uneven edges.

Lenses Curved pieces of glass, which make objects look bigger or smaller.

Limestone A kind of rock.

Logo A design or mark that is put on a product to tell you something.

Long-lasting Can be used for a long time before it breaks or wears out.

Magnifying glass Lens in a holder used to look at small objects - it makes them appear bigger.

Material Something out of which other objects can be made.

Microscope A machine with powerful glass lenses that makes very tiny objects look bigger.

Molten Melted.

Moulds Shapes that liquid glass is poured into to make glass objects in those shapes.

Mouldy Food that has gone bad. It is harmful to eat.

Natural Comes from the Earth, plants or animals.

Opaque A material you cannot see through but which still allows light through.

Optical fibres Very thin threads of glass, which light can shine along.

Ornaments Objects used to decorate a home.

Recycling Using a material again.

Rot To go soft and crumbly.

Safety glass Glass that is stronger than ordinary glass.

Stained glass Glass made in different colours.

Transparent See-through.

Waterproof Does not let water pass through.

Index